The Black Drum

The Black Drum

Adam Pottle

PLAYWRIGHTS CANADA PRESS
Toronto

First edition: April 2024
Printed and bound in Canada by Imprimerie Gauvin, Gatineau

Jacket art and design by Maryam Hafizirad
Author photo by Tenille Campbell, Sweetmoon Photography

Playwrights Canada Press
202-269 Richmond St. W., Toronto, ON M5V 1X1
416.703.0013 | info@playwrightscanada.com | www.playwrightscanada.com

LIBRARY AND ARCHIVES CANADA CATALOGUING IN PUBLICATION
Title: The black drum / Adam Pottle.
Names: Pottle, Adam, author.
Identifiers: Canadiana (print) 2024032126X | Canadiana (ebook) 20240321294 | ISBN 9780369104861 (softcover) | ISBN 9780369104878 (PDF) | ISBN 9780369104885 (EPUB)
Subjects: LCGFT: Musicals. | LCGFT: Drama.
Classification: LCC PS8631.07746 B53 2024 | DDC C812/.6—dc23

Playwrights Canada Press staff work across Turtle Island, on Treaty 7, Treaty 13, and Treaty 20 territories, which are the current and ancestral homes of the Anishinaabe Nations (Ojibwe / Chippewa, Odawa, Potawatomi, Algonquin, Saulteaux, Nipissing, and Mississauga / Michi Saagiig), the Blackfoot Confederacy (Kainai, Piikani, and Siksika), nêhiyaw, Sioux, Stoney Nakoda, Tsuut'ina, Wendat, and members of the Haudenosaunee Confederacy (Mohawk, Oneida, Onondaga, Cayuga, Seneca, and Tuscarora), as well as Metis and Inuit peoples. It always was and always will be Indigenous land.

We acknowledge the financial support of the Canada Council for the Arts, the Ontario Arts Council (OAC), Ontario Creates, the Government of Ontario, and the Government of Canada for our publishing activities.

Canada Council for the Arts | Conseil des arts du Canada
ONTARIO ARTS COUNCIL
CONSEIL DES ARTS DE L'ONTARIO
an Ontario government agency
un organisme du gouvernement de l'Ontario
ONTARIO CREATES | ONTARIO CRÉATIF
Canada
Ontario

For the cast and crew. Your brilliant work illuminated something in me, and just as you all held me that day in Reims, I hold you all close in my heart.

Affirmations: An Introduction to *The Black Drum*

Adam Pottle

In the Deaf community, one typically presents one's credentials—that is, one's background—upon meeting other Deaf people. My credentials are as follows: I was born Deaf but grew up in a hearing family. Like many Deaf people around the world, I had to conform to my family's way of doing things, which meant using hearing aids and enduring speech therapy. As a result, my conception of music was based in sound, and while I enjoyed and still enjoy music, my relationship with it was and remains complicated. Whenever I listened to music as a kid—KISS, Def Leppard, The Eagles, Cher, Garth Brooks, Headpins, Cheap Trick, Alannah Myles, and Bryan Adams were standards in our house—I had to listen around the gap in my experiences, the gap of growing up without a community. I never went to Deaf schools. I seldom if ever hung out with other Deaf kids. My access to music was tilted, indirect. Just about everything was like that: television, movies, conversations. Outside of books, I received almost everything second-hand, through captions or notes or awkward gestures or crackling microphones or repeated jokes. My world was visual. Kinetic. A potential that I couldn't quite gain simmered beneath the sounds. It would take decades for me to finally tap into that potential.

*

In 2016, Joanne Cripps, then the executive director of the Canadian Cultural Society of the Deaf (CCSD) in Toronto, approached me and asked if I'd be interested in writing the story for a Deaf musical. At the time, I'd only recently begun learning American Sign Language. My first play *Ultrasound* had been produced that May and explored a marriage between a Deaf man and a hard-of-hearing woman. Blissfully ignorant of the enormity of the task ahead, I said yes immediately.

About a week later, after the idea had finally sunk into my stubborn brain, I realized what I'd gotten myself into. My brain filled with rubber; my heart prickled with anxiety. Every time I sat down to type out a line or jot down a note, my hands were stifled.

How does one write the story for a Deaf musical? What is a Deaf musical?

While there have been and are many Deaf musicians—Beethoven, Sean Forbes, Bob Hiltermann, Evelyn Glennie, among others—and while there have been musicals featuring Deaf performers, such as 2015's *Spring Awakening*, there had never been a play revolving around Deaf music. That is, Signed Music.

As Joan, the protagonist of *The Black Drum*, suggests, Signed Music is not notes written on scales or plucked on strings or played on keys. It is not a mere translation of song lyrics. It is wholly organic. It grows out of the body—specifically, the Deaf body. It incorporates dance, physical theatre, and visual poetry. It exists in and emanates out of the flesh and the bones. It does not simply occupy space; it churns it, cracks it, irradiates it with movement and expression. It takes Sign Language and amplifies and exaggerates and invigorates it into visual music.

But I didn't know this at the time. It had never been defined or used in service of a story before. In creating this play, I was, along with the cast and crew, helping to define what Signed Music was, along with challenging accepted definitions of music. Music is not just something we hear. It is something we can see. Something we can feel.

So the question remained. How do I write a story for a Deaf musical?

I tried using my writerly bag of tricks. I'd published books before, so I resorted to what I knew. I jotted notes. I wrote snippets of dialogue. I presented a loose outline to the CCSD of a dark fantasy story, which they approved, then spent the next two years working through various drafts, all of them full of holes. I chose a dark fantasy because I was fed up with realism, and because Deaf people seldom appear in fantasy stories. My ultimate goal was to create a Deaf mythology. But my background as a poet and novelist and English teacher budged up against the play's core. The one play I had written had not prepared me in any way for this endeavour. Verbosity would not work here. Written and spoken English would not work here. This script, I realized, would be a blueprint, not something performed verbatim, as in typical theatre practice; I'd provide the storyline and motivations for the characters, and the cast and crew would translate the dialogue and compose the music based on the situations I created. I had high expectations of myself, as I do with any project I take on, but I had no idea how to write a story that not only cohered with this new conception of music but bolstered it and drove it to entertaining and exhilarating heights. I wanted to give the cast and crew the substance they needed.

I grew frustrated. I couldn't imagine it. By undertaking this play, we were not just telling a story or subverting the way the world views music. We were, in a small way, challenging the foundations of theatre practice.

In August 2018, I flew to Toronto to work with the cast at honing the story and experimenting with Signed Music. There were seven adult characters and three youth performers. Our entire cast was Deaf, as were the director and several crew members. With such a large cast, we had to ensure the production was accessible at every single level, which meant interpreters. Several hearing crew members showed tremendous commitment and learned American Sign Language. The solidarity was astonishing.

I enjoyed everyone's company. The cast and crew were brilliant. But the play still wasn't there. The story lurched rather than flowed. The characters were made of tin. I felt I was disappointing everyone.

✷

At the same time I was working on the script for *The Black Drum*, I was preparing my memoir for publication. It was titled *Voice* and examined the impact being Deaf had on my imagination. In the past, I called writing this memoir performing a vivisection on myself. That's untrue. Even though I explored childhood memories of being fitted for hearing aids, of sitting in class and misunderstanding my peers, and of being seen as less, I maintained a safe distance from the material. I wrote the memoir from behind a veil of sarcasm. That was a mistake, because it prevented me from telling the real truth about my experiences. That veil prevented me from seeing the impact of my parents' decision to keep me from going to Deaf school. It prevented me from realizing that I should have learned Sign Language and sought friendships with Deaf people much sooner.

The truth was that, for most of my life, I'd harboured in my heart a bristling, screeching ball of black poison I eventually came to see as internalized ableism. I'd spent so much of my life trying to appear hearing, which meant denying and suppressing this integral part of myself. As a child, I had problems with the word "Deaf." I never called myself that. The word was too blunt, too true. I used the words "hard-of-hearing" instead. To call myself Deaf was, in my mind, admitting defeat.

Commensurately, my problem with *The Black Drum* was I was approaching it like a hearing person. I needed to approach it as a Deaf person. But I couldn't do that until I saw myself as a Deaf person. I needed to fully embrace the power and beauty of being Deaf, but I didn't know how.

✷

In December 2018, I flew to Oslo, Norway, to work with *The Black Drum*'s director, Mira Zuckermann. At our first meeting on a brisk winter morning, we both agreed that the script was inadequate, so I holed myself up in my tiny hotel room and started the script again from the beginning.

During the day, I would visit Mira's theatre, Teater Manu, to discuss my progress, and in the evening, between writing sessions, I walked the streets of Oslo. One evening, I visited the National Gallery, which houses some of the most famous artworks of the 20th century. On the gallery's expansive second level, I stepped into a large, beautifully appointed room. Rich, thick moulding. Hardwood floors. The paintings hanging on the walls were all gorgeous and evocative, yet they all seemed to be leading to something, like the lights on either side of a runway. At the far end of the room, occupying the middle of the wall, was Edvard Munch's *The Scream*. I stared at it. I'd seen this painting a thousand times on screens and T-shirts. I straightened and smoothed out my coat as though I'd locked eyes with a celebrity. The figure in the painting gripped their face with both hands. Their voice was silent. Or was it? Was the scream supposed to occur inside my head? What was it supposed to sound like? Or was it meant to be sound at all? Was the figure's expression and body language and the world on fire in the background all the scream I needed? The painting, it seemed, was reflecting back at me, and with uncanny precision, my own internal conflict with ableism, presenting me with my own Nietzschean abyss.

I kept working on the play. The next night, I walked down a cobblestone street and came to a beautiful square. There was an ice rink, a Ferris wheel rigged with bright purple lights, and a gaggle of food vendors selling sausages and donuts. Surrounding the square were Rolex dealers, hotels, and restaurants. I bought a sausage on a bun, sat down and ate, then began walking back to my hotel.

As I rounded a corner, a crowd of hundreds of people marched toward me, accompanied by police officers on horseback. They carried candles. I had no way to pass them, so I stepped to the side and waited. The crowd gathered outside the nearby Grand Hotel. Up on the balcony, a man and a woman—both stately and elegant— emerged and waved to the crowd.

I approached a police officer. "What's happening?" I said.

I concentrated on her lips and deciphered the word "Nobel."

I glanced back up at the two figures on the balcony. The Nobel Peace Prize was awarded in Oslo every year, and I was looking up at that year's recipients, Dr. Denis Mukwege and Nadia Murad.

Mukwege and Murad smiled and waved to the crowd. The scene had an incredible, storybook quality. My limbs tingled. My heart glowed. I'd never been this close to a Stanley Cup winner, much less a Nobel winner. To see this unity, this celebration, was a beautiful privilege.

After five days of working for nearly eighteen hours a day, I gave Mira the new script, completely rewritten from scratch, detailing the journey of Joan, a Deaf woman wrestling with grief who must realize the power of her own voice. Mira's response, delivered in Norwegian Sign Language and translated by her sister, Sølvi: "This'll work."

*

The Black Drum premiered at Soulpepper Theatre in Toronto in June 2019, as a co-production with the Canadian Cultural Society of the Deaf. In the months leading up to the production, the cast and crew had taken my script and fleshed it out during rehearsals and workshops in Banff and Toronto. The actors, directors, and choreographers built their compositions out of the story I provided; in the process, they created an entirely new sign to describe Signed Music. The sign goes like this: stack your fists knuckle to knuckle before your chest, the right knuckles facing left, the left knuckles facing right. As you raise both hands, open them up and twist them away from your body, as though you're releasing something from inside you.

Because I live in Saskatoon, I couldn't attend rehearsals, so when I arrived on opening night, I had no idea what to expect.

In the same way that *The Scream* reflected my internalized ableism back at me, the play was an affirmation of Deaf beauty. The actors' movements and heart, the designers' artistry—all of it amazed me. By the end of the play, I'd broken down into tears. Through their stunning work, the performers had given me permission to embrace my Deaf self.

That affirmation was heightened exponentially when, a month later, I attended the Clin d'Oeil festival in Reims, France. This festival is the world's biggest Deaf arts festival, and *The Black Drum* was chosen as a featured show. Seeing thousands of Deaf people communicating in multiple Sign Languages was like discovering an entirely new world, a world I had been part of all along but was unable to step into.

I never slept the entire four days in Reims. My body was humming from the anxiety of exuviation, of becoming something new. Every nerve quivered. My hands shook constantly.

One morning, after spending the night squeezing my eyes shut and trying to will myself to sleep, I rose from my bed and went for a walk. It was 5 am. No one else walked the cobbled streets.

I turned down a road and walked toward the Notre-Dame de Reims cathedral, which stood at the far end, a hulking mass of stone and glass. The sun had begun to rise behind the cathedral; the yellow light framed it with an incredible saintly glow.

I sat on a bench in front of the cathedral. I was all alone. I had this magnificent sight all to myself.

I waited for my anxiety to quiet and tried to luxuriate in the beauty of this sight, but my anxiety persisted. My skin was shedding. I was raw, becoming something new. I bristled as the sun's light stroked my hand; even the gentlest touches hurt when your skin is peeled. At the time, I didn't know what I was going through, but, like the workers who built the cathedral over the course of a century, I knew I had to endure. I had to continue the work.

✷

In many ways, Joan's journey through the black and white fantasy world is my own. Joan must work her way through the darkness and embrace the music, the beauty, lying dormant within herself. She must embrace love and fellowship, or risk being sucked into a maelstrom of confusion and distress. She must confront the black poison pulsing within her, which takes the guise of the horrific antagonist, the Minister.

Everything that's happened in the last several years has yielded indelible images. The play, the actors, the crew, *The Scream*, the crowd with the candles, the Nobel laureates, the sun rising behind the cathedral—all of them are golden pieces of affirmation. As I continue to develop and create from and within my Deaf self, I continue to experience that affirmation. I become less confused and more confident.

For sparking this affirmation, I must thank several people:

For their sensitive and intelligent work, and for showing me the wondrous possibilities of Deaf creation, I thank the cast and crew of *The Black Drum*, especially Mira Zuckermann, who was a firm but gentle guiding hand.

For their support, I thank all those who bought a ticket to see the play, and all those who buy or sign out a copy of this book.

For her patient instruction, I thank my ASL teacher, Janet Dittrick.

For their friendship, I thank my fellow Deaf artists Maryam Hafizirad, Ebony Gooden, Courage Bacchus, and Chris Dodd.

For their love, I thank my wife Deborah and my goldendoodle Valkyrie.

That black poison remains inside me. But with each day it becomes more diluted. I hope that readers of this book (and, hopefully, audience members at future productions) receive the same affirmation I did.

Notes

The script that follows was first revised in November 2019 and again in October 2023. I replaced the original production's Signed Music piece titled "Money" with a piece titled "Celebrate." It suits the story much better.

Because Signed Music exists primarily on the stage rather than the page, the English versions of all compositions are provided in the text.

While the script is written in English, the play is performed in native sign language. The intention of *The Black Drum* is to celebrate Deaf Life using sign language and Signed Music.

Permission to produce the play as it was first performed in June and July 2019 must be obtained from both the playwright and the original producer, the Canadian Cultural Society of the Deaf. Productions wishing to create their own Signed Music need obtain permission from only the playwright.

To coincide with the premiere production, the Canadian Cultural Society of the Deaf published a youth activities guide, which can be found at https://deafculturecentre.ca/resources/documents/ (Canadian Cultural Society of the Deaf. (2021). *The Black Drum*

Signed Musical: Behind the Scenes Youth Activities Guide. [Cripps, J. Project Manager; Small, A. Content Manager], Toronto, Ontario: Canadian Cultural Society of the Deaf).

The Black Drum was commissioned and first produced by the Canadian Cultural Society of the Deaf and presented by Soulpepper Theatre Company at the Young Centre for Performing Arts, Toronto, from June 15 to 29, 2019, with the following cast and creative team:

Minister: Bob Hiltermann
Joan: Dawn Jani Birley
Bree and Butterfly: Yan Liu
Oscar and Bulldog: Daniel Durant
Squib: Natasha C. Bacchus
Ava: Corinna Den Dekker
Karen: Agata Wisny
Ballet dancers: Jaelyn Russell-Lillie, Sita Weereatne, and Abbey Jackson-Bell

Director: Mira Zuckermann
Producer / Executive Director: Joanne Cripps
Director, Cross Cultural Development / Research: Anita Small
Assistant Director: Jack Volpe
Production Manager: Sally Roberts
Stage Manager: Sandi Becker
Assistant Stage Manager: Seren Brooke Lannon
Set & Props Designer: Ken MacKenzie
Lighting Designer: Chris Malkowski
Costume Designer: Ruth Albertyn
Makeup and Assistant Costume Designer: Maryam Hafizirad

Sound Designer: Adam Harendorf
Drummer: Dimitri Kanaris
Sound Assistant: Jason Cripps
Motion Capture Designer: Chris Joslin
Video & Projection Designer: Laura Warren
Signed Music Specialist: Pamela Witcher
Choreographer and Movement Director: Patricia Allison
Technical Director: JT Pickering
Student Ballet Instructors: Jeffrey Baker and Katie Harkins
Fight Director: Geoff Scovell
Student Ballet Facilitator: Gwen Fischer
Head of Wardrobe: Negar Nemati
Head Costume Builder: Melanie McNeill
Wardrobe Assistant: Harpreet Kaur
Makeup Artist/Mentor: Angela McQueen
Head of Props: Emily Butters
ASL Masters: Ron Hall and Helen Pizzacalla
Communications / Audience Engagement Manager: Catherine Joell MacKinnon
Marketing and Promotion Art & Design: Maryam Hafizirad
Media Team Lead: Ely Lyonblum
Communications / Audience Engagement: Katie O'Connor
Research: Jody Cripps
ASL / English Interpreters: Peggy Zehr, Rosalie Vissers, Sharon Pardy, Sheila Johnston, Tegan McFarlane, April Holtom, and Victoria Dwight
Resident Dramaturge: Tine Thomasson
Assistant Dramaturge: Sølvi R. Zuckermann
NSL / English Interpreter: Siri Gjellan, Christina Bruland, Marianne Larosi, and Anne Strodal
Audio Recording Voice Actors: Raquel Duffy and Diego Matamoros
Audio Recording Voice Direction: Nathalie Toriel
Audio Recording Engineer: Rachel Johnstone

Characters

MINISTER: a monster and ruler of the In-Between Land
JOAN: a performer grieving her wife
BREE: Joan's friend
OSCAR: Joan's friend
KAREN: Joan's wife, deceased
TREE: a sentient part of the In-Between Land
SQUIB: the Minister's henchperson
AVA: an inhabitant of the In-Between Land and the kids' teacher
BULLDOG: Joan's tattoo come to life in the In-Between Land (looks like Oscar)
BUTTERFLY: Joan's tattoo come to life in the In-Between Land (looks like Bree)
KIDS: dancing inhabitants of the In-Between Land

Scene One

A dark, sinister landscape. Barren, with gnarled black trees.

A slow drumbeat.

The black trees in the background clench their branches like fingers.

Spotlight on the MINISTER, *an enormous figure wearing a black hooded robe. He has a pale, ghoulish face.*

Black Heart

MINISTER: My black heart is beautiful
Death is beautiful
This dark world is mine
I control you all!
(long) There's no music
No laughter, no happiness
No colour, no friendship
No freedom
No love!
This black heart is beautiful
This black heart is perfect
You're all worthless

My black heart is beautiful
Sadness is good, anger is good!
You'll never be free!
Never be free!
Never be free!

The MINISTER, *drumbeat, and sinister landscape fade away.*

Scene Two

A cemetery.

Headstones. A cloudy day.

JOAN, a thirty-year-old Deaf woman, stands at the grave of KAREN, her dead wife.

JOAN has several tattoos up and down her arms. She wears a vest with yellow, red, and green pins.

Her friends and roommates, BREE and OSCAR, stand a short ways behind her, waiting. OSCAR fidgets impatiently.

JOAN: I had an audition today. Same question: "Where's your instrument?" My body's my instrument. No one gets it.

OSCAR: *(to BREE)* When will she let go?

BREE: Stop.

JOAN: *(to the grave)* I miss you. I feel empty inside. I got a new tattoo—a butterfly. Beautiful, like you. And my bulldog—full of strength to keep me going.

OSCAR: *(to BREE)* Depressing. When I die, I want people to party. Dancing, drinking.

BREE: I'll be dancing when you die.

OSCAR starts dancing.

OSCAR: Our skeletons can dance together.

BREE: Stop it. Think of Joan . . .

As OSCAR performs his song, BREE scuffles with him as she tries to cut him off.

As OSCAR performs this song, gleeful skeletons dance around him. Champagne bottles pop open; party favours go off, spraying confetti everywhere.

Celebrate

OSCAR: One, two, three, four . . .
Let go . . .
Dance!
Drink!
Celebrate!
Skeletons, dance!
Let go!
Celebrate life!

JOAN notices OSCAR's song. A look of contempt crosses her face.

Dance forward!
Leave your worries behind!
Don't mourn
Don't grieve
Be happy
Celebrate!
Live your best life!
Skeletons, dance!

BREE: You're like a child.

JOAN: That's enough!

BREE: Sorry. We'll meet you in the car, okay?

BREE and OSCAR exit.

JOAN: *(to the grave)* Uh, Oscar and Bree, still scuffling with each other. I'm still living with them. I don't like being alone.

KAREN—really, KAREN's ghost—emerges behind Joan. KAREN wears a colourful outfit, but her face and body language are mournful, despairing.

KAREN glides past JOAN, reaching out for her. JOAN seems to sense her but doesn't see her. KAREN drifts off the stage. JOAN glances around but sees nothing.

(points to her chest) I'll always have the tattoo of you here, always close to my heart. I don't know how to move on, Karen.

JOAN kneels down, crying.

I feel you all the time. Tell me what to do. Please.

Scene Three

The trees and the sky begin to blacken. The cemetery fades away. A drumbeat rumbles.

JOAN *peers around and jars, startled, frightened.*

A dark spiral develops and whirls. A black tunnel opens, enveloping JOAN.

A bizarre world forms around JOAN. *Trees acquire the shape of clenching hands. Everything is black and white.*

This is the sinister black landscape in Scene One. This is the In-Between Land.

The drumbeat fades.

The tunnel shrinks, then closes.

JOAN *wanders from one side of the stage to the other.*

A tree clenches and seizes—and begins signing. Its movements are aggressive and grim.

TREE: He will chew you up! Chew you up and swallow you! Get away!

Thunder cracks. Black lightning rips across the sky.

The tree seizes as though in pain.

SQUIB, *the* MINISTER*'s lieutenant, comes in the other side.*

SQUIB: Stop! By this black heart, I must take you away. The Minister is waiting for you.

SQUIB chases JOAN to the edge of the stage.

JOAN: Who are you?

SQUIB: I'm Squib, a soldier for the Minister.

SQUIB grabs JOAN by the neck and hauls her off stage.

Scene Four

A bleak wooded area. Burnt trees. Dismal mountains.

AVA, a young teacher, works with a group of KIDS. Their clothing is a gloomy black.

The KIDS perform a dance number. Their movements are stiff, almost robotic.

JOAN runs onto the stage, panting, glancing over her shoulder.

AVA and the KIDS edge away from JOAN.

JOAN: Where am I? Why do they chase me?

AVA: *(to the KIDS)* Quick. Go home.

The KIDS exit, marching like robotic soldiers.

We should get away. You're wearing colours. It's dangerous to be out in the open. You must leave before the Minister sees you.

AVA sees someone off stage.

Hide!

JOAN and AVA hide behind a bush.

Two figures march on stage: a BULLDOG and a BUTTERFLY. They bicker with each other.

The BULLDOG *looks a lot like* OSCAR, *and the* BUTTERFLY *looks a lot like* BREE.

Celebrate (Reprise)

BULLDOG: Celebrate! Celebrate!
There is no death
Skeletons, dance!
I'm the big dog, the bulldog—

BUTTERFLY: We need to find Joan.

JOAN *steps out from behind the bush.* AVA *follows.*

BULLDOG *goes to* JOAN *and smells* AVA.

BULLDOG: Who's this?

JOAN *shields* AVA.

BUTTERFLY: We won't hurt you.

(to JOAN*)* Don't we look familiar?

AVA: You know them?

JOAN: They're my tattoos. My bulldog and my butterfly.

(to BULLDOG*)* You look like Oscar.

BULLDOG: In the flesh.

The BULLDOG runs up to JOAN and nuzzles her, the way a dog would. JOAN pets him; the BULLDOG grins and shakes his leg.

BULLDOG: Who's your friend?

AVA: I'm Ava. Why are you here?

BUTTERFLY: We've been waiting for you.

The drum rumbles. The world shakes.

JOAN: Why does the ground shake?

AVA: That's the heart of this land, the Black Drum. The Minister uses his dark magic to keep the Drum black. As long as it's black, he has power over all of us.

JOAN: Am I dead? Is this death?

BUTTERFLY: *(points off stage)* That area is real life.

(points in other direction) That area is the dead world. Both of them are here together, in your mind. An in-between world.

JOAN: Why have you two come to life, but not Karen?

BULLDOG: Karen's dead.

The BUTTERFLY smacks him.

BUTTERFLY: We haven't seen her. I'm sorry.

The ground rumbles. Something approaches.

AVA *grabs* JOAN *and exits. The* BUTTERFLY *and the* BULLDOG *exit to the opposite side.*

Scene Five

Same place.

The trees clench. The landscape shakes.

The MINISTER *emerges, pulling* KAREN *as though by an invisible rope.*

Lightning crackles across the sky as the MINISTER *tortures* KAREN. KAREN*'s body buckles, folds.*

MINISTER: I smell wet dog. No room for colour. No music.
No voice. Except mine. This is my land.
My responsibility. No one escapes me.

Abyss

MINISTER: See the abyss!
The black hole calls—
There's no hope, no comfort
True peace is black, empty
Love is not worth it
No light touches me!
Love is an illusion!
I eat light
You're mine! You belong to me!
For true peace, you must give up
Close your heart, close your eyes
Love is dark, love is an abyss . . .

The MINISTER *drags* KAREN *off stage with him.*

Just as they exit, JOAN *sees* KAREN *and chases after her.*

As JOAN *chases after* KAREN, *a powerful force like an invisible wall pushes* JOAN *away, closing her off from* KAREN.

The darkness subsides. The thunder and lightning stop. The trees relax.

JOAN *crumples and cries. The* BUTTERFLY *comforts* JOAN, *holding her.*

JOAN: Her hands were bound. Did you see her eyes?

As the BUTTERFLY *performs her song, gorgeous shapes and colours surround her, including caterpillars and butterflies—*

No Cocoon Can Hold Me

BUTTERFLY: When I was a baby
When I was a caterpillar
Wrapped in a silk blanket
Wrapped up snug and tight
I dreamed of open air
The wind on my face
Flying with the wind
The world lying below me
My cocoon
My prison
My shackles
I dreamed of hope
I grew—
I changed—

I broke free—
Spread my wings
Show the world my colour!
Show the world my beauty!
No cocoon can hold me
No prison can hold my colour
Colour flies
Beauty soars
There's always hope
You can escape

The shapes and colours fade.

Scene Six

Same place.

JOAN tries to run to the valley and follow the MINISTER. AVA and BULLDOG stop her. JOAN cries.

JOAN: Karen's in hell. This is hell!

AVA: Who was that?

BULLDOG: Joan's dead wife. She was eaten.

BUTTERFLY: She had an infection.

JOAN: She can't have peace, even in death.

BUTTERFLY: We can't do anything yet. We need a plan.

AVA: We need music and colour to make the Drum beat stronger and faster. Then the black will fade away, and we'll all be free. You can help us.

JOAN: How?

BUTTERFLY: Use your music.

JOAN: My music isn't strong enough.

BULLDOG: Music won't kill a monster like that. We need force. We can't stay here, or we'll die like those ruined trees.

BUTTERFLY: It has to be Joan. Only she can set Karen free.

AVA: You need to travel to the Minister, to the Drum. Down in the valley.

JOAN: What music do I do?

BUTTERFLY: Do your audition piece. Find it in your heart.

As JOAN *performs this piece, beautiful colours and shapes arc across the sky, like meteors, or northern lights. The trees awaken and dance and sway.*

What Is Music?

JOAN: What is music?
Not black notes
Not plucked strings
Not pushed keys
It's rhythm
It's colour
It's a paintbrush
It's dancing
A ticking clock
The water in the ocean
The birds in the air
The wind in the trees
Feel the beat
See my music
Feel my music
Everything is music
My heartbeat is music

The blood in my veins is music
My body is my instrument
I dance to my own music
See my music!
Feel my music!

The trees relax. The colours fade.

AVA: *(excited)* More!

JOAN: Is that enough?

BUTTERFLY: You can do it. Bulldog and I will distract the Minister and try to get Karen. You go to the Drum.

JOAN: I want to get Karen.

BUTTERFLY: You'll see her soon.

BULLDOG: I'm not distracting him—I'm going to kill him, like this.

The BULLDOG makes clawing and stomping motions.

AVA: I want to help.

JOAN: No. Protect the kids.

(to BUTTERFLY) Do I get to stay with Karen when it's over?

BUTTERFLY: No. You'll save her, but you'll need to let her go.

BULLDOG: Yeah. Let her go.

JOAN: I can't. I've tried.

BUTTERFLY: She's a piece of you. Just like us. We need to go. The Minister probably saw those colours. I know you will fight him.

BULLDOG: I'm hungry. Should we eat first? Never tackle a villain on an empty stomach.

The BUTTERFLY *grabs the* BULLDOG *by the collar and leads him off stage.*

AVA: Don't leave me. You're colourful. I want to be beautiful like you.

JOAN *gives* AVA *a yellow pin from her vest.*

JOAN: Yellow.

AVA: Yellow.

Yellow, purple, and green shimmer in the sky like the northern lights.

JOAN *smiles at the colours, then strides off stage.* AVA *holds the pin to her chest, then goes off the opposite direction.*

The trees relax. The colours fade.

Scene Seven

A field of black and white flowers.

The flowers fold inward as the MINISTER *approaches.*

The MINISTER *marches on stage, yanking* KAREN *along on the invisible rope.*

Colours spark in the sky, leaving streaks on the air.

The MINISTER *sees the colours and stops.* KAREN *pulls against him.*

KAREN: Why are you doing this?

MINISTER: Demonstration of strength.

KAREN: You don't know what strength is.

MINISTER: I can do what I want. I'll destroy your heart. Must keep my world black.

KAREN: Destruction, anger . . . that's not strength.

MINISTER: You see those colours? Colour weakens me. Your friends must be destroyed. The colour must be torn, burned, blackened.

KAREN: Compassion, love, sharing. That's strength.

MINISTER: Love is an illusion. Death is the greatest force in the world.

KAREN: Life is the greatest force. People laugh. They kiss. They cry.

They make love. They create art.

The flowers in the field tremble.

MINISTER: Death is necessary.

KAREN: Death destroys worlds. It separates people. Know how I know? I'm not with my wife right now.

As KAREN performs this song, the sky alights with purple and blue. Comets streak across the sky.

The MINISTER strikes at the colours like a child lashing out at insects.

Without Her

KAREN: I'm empty
Cold without her
Her eyes are windows
To a new galaxy

As KAREN continues performing her song, JOAN emerges in the distance, searching the land. They don't see each other . . . but JOAN works her way closer to KAREN.

Her kiss feels like home
My heart is full always
Her beauty burns within me
She is a burning star
She carries brilliant love for all
She is strong

JOAN: My love is too big
Can't keep it inside
Can't forget her
I miss her always

KAREN and JOAN mirror each other's movements without actually seeing each other, without realizing just how connected they are.

KAREN & JOAN: Life is empty
Life is cold without her
We create a world together
Our own planet
I can't keep it inside
My love is too big
My light is too bright

The MINISTER is fed up. He slashes at the sky, grey lightning shuddering across the expanse, cutting KAREN's song off.

KAREN buckles from the impact. JOAN runs off, continuing her search.

MINISTER: You'll be together soon. In death.

The BULLDOG leaps out and bites and tackles the MINISTER. The MINISTER pushes the BULLDOG off.

The BUTTERFLY runs over to KAREN and tries to undo her bonds. The MINISTER throws the BULLDOG off and jabs his hand at the BUTTERFLY.

Lightning cuts across the sky.

The BUTTERFLY seizes with pain and then kicks the MINISTER in the face.

The flowers in the field seize, then fall limp, dead.

Bad Dog, Good Dog

BULLDOG: Run, run, run
Bite, bite, bite
Drool, drool, drool
You all see me as bad
That I'm a bad dog
But I'm your friend
I cherish you, I protect you
I look bad, but I'm open
I'm deep, I'm friendly
I have a big heart
I'm a good dog
I'm a good dog!

The MINISTER stands and, with a ferocious movement, gains control of the BULLDOG, the BUTTERFLY, and KAREN.

Their hands bind together, and the MINISTER leads them by an invisible rope as they exit.

Scene Eight

A shady area of the woods.

The KIDS *have gathered around* AVA. *They move with much more freedom and joy; their gloomy clothes have been lightened with vibrant colours.*

AVA *holds up the pin* JOAN *gave her.*

AVA: Yellow.

KIDS: Yellow.

AVA: Do you want more colour like this?

KIDS: Yes!

AVA: We have a chance to change the world, to give the world more colour, more hope. We must help. We must use our secret music.

AVA *stands and gestures for the* KIDS *to stand.* AVA *and the* KIDS *perform together. Their movements are rhythmic, beautiful, showing each person's individual music.*

Voice

AVA & KIDS: My world—
All ruined, destroyed, turned to dust
But grief . . .
But pain . . .
That's all finished

Fear and shame?
That's finished
Oppression?
That's finished!
Our voices live!
We'll save this world!
We'll love
We'll laugh, we'll dance
We're brave!

A thick rumble. The sky darkens; lightning flashes.

The KIDS *run to* AVA*; they all huddle together, then run off stage.*

Scene Nine

A soft drumbeat arises, like a dying heart.

A ceremonial place in the heart of a valley. A sacred place, like Stonehenge.

Giant statues surround the area. The statues are dark, genderless humanoids, like Oscar statues.

SQUIB *patrols the area. She mocks the statues and performs her song for them.*

Oppressor's Lament

SQUIB: The Minister controls
He chokes
He chases
I'm all alone—why?
I must survive
He oppresses me
He oppresses you
I hate his black heart
I give my heart, my heartbeat
I give it all
I have no choice
But I must survive

JOAN *emerges cautiously.*

(snaps to attention) Go away.

JOAN: I need to get to the Drum.

SQUIB: Nobody gets to the Drum. The Minister's on his way.

JOAN: I need to save my wife.

SQUIB: Look at them. They all had to save someone. Look what happened to them.

JOAN: Are you alone?

SQUIB: Being alone's better than being dead.

JOAN: My wife is out there hurting. Being alone's not worth it. I know.

SQUIB: He'll kill me if I don't stop you.

> *Just as SQUIB's about to give in to JOAN, the MINISTER enters with KAREN, BUTTERFLY, and BULLDOG.*

> *With his magic, the MINISTER seizes control of JOAN. JOAN stiffens.*

MINISTER: *(to SQUIB)* You little weakling.

> *The BULLDOG shakes loose from his bonds and claws at the MINISTER; the MINISTER forces him back.*

> *The BUTTERFLY attacks the MINISTER, but to no avail.*

> *With a sweeping gesture, the MINISTER takes control over everyone. He sets KAREN spinning, like a ballerina in a*

music box. The others all rest on their knees, hunched over, like robots without batteries.

AVA enters. The MINISTER advances toward her.

AVA: We want colour!

The MINISTER slashes at AVA; AVA recoils, but keeps coming . . .

We want our power back!

The MINISTER slashes at her again. AVA presses on:

We want freedom!

With a hard slash through the air, the MINISTER subdues AVA; she joins the others, hunched over, almost lifeless.

The MINISTER commands SQUIB to fetch him the Black Drum.

SQUIB enters with the Black Drum, an enormous instrument. One strike on it is like a punch in the gut.

The MINISTER picks up his mallets and begins playing the Drum: JOAN, the BUTTERFLY, the BULLDOG, and AVA all rise to their feet. They are all under the MINISTER's control.

The MINISTER waves someone in front of him: one of the KIDS enters, her hands bound behind her back.

The MINISTER controls the KID's movements with the Drum, making the KID do what he wants, demonstrating his strength.

The MINISTER tortures the KID with his power, then waves the KID off stage. He plays a fast, harsh beat, causing JOAN, the BULLDOG, the BUTTERFLY, and AVA to shake violently. KAREN remains separate, spinning like a ghostly ballerina.

The MINISTER finishes playing. His prisoners fall, exhausted, in pain.

Control

MINISTER: They're all good for nothing
You all! You're all stuck, imprisoned, locked up
I'm the law here
I'm nature here
I'm in control
The world is on fire, upside down
If you stay, soon you'll have nothing to worry about
You all will follow me!
My Black Drum, my high power
Give yourselves to the blackness
Give yourselves to me!

The MINISTER leaves, eyeing SQUIB, as though questioning her loyalty.

SQUIB takes the Black Drum away, but before she takes it off stage, she picks up a mallet and hits the Drum once, waking up the BULLDOG, the BUTTERFLY, AVA, and JOAN.

JOAN goes to KAREN, who continues to spin slowly, as though in an entirely other dimension. JOAN waves her hand in KAREN's face; KAREN doesn't see her.

JOAN: What's wrong with her?

BUTTERFLY: We can't be weak. We need you. Help us. It's about you. You need to let go. You have the colours. You have the music to beat the Minister. Go on.

The BUTTERFLY and JOAN come together—and begin to sign:

BUTTERFLY & JOAN: Love . . . love . . . open the fire . . . use your voice . . .

JOAN begins to take off on her own . . .

Love Is Freedom

JOAN: Love is freedom
Open your wings
Freedom is my voice
Freedom is my beauty
My voice is love
Love is strength
The world in my hand!
Love is life
Laughter flies like butterflies
Tears make rivers
Taking us forward
Love is freedom!

The MINISTER enters, shocked at his prisoners' defiance.

The drumbeat thunders.

The MINISTER and JOAN approach the front of the stage.

The BULLDOG, the BUTTERFLY, AVA, and SQUIB dance behind them. It's a showdown between JOAN and the MINISTER.

The drumbeat picks up speed . . .

The MINISTER slashes at JOAN—

But JOAN blocks it with her sign:

(tentative) Life . . .

The MINISTER stumbles, as though smacked in the head. He slashes at her again.

(stronger) Life!

JOAN advances toward the MINISTER.

As they battle and JOAN gains strength, galaxies of colour spark across the sky.

The trees and grass begin to turn green. Purple lightning crackles. Comets streak brightly. The flowers turn red and pink and white. The statues move and smile.

Continues "Love Is Freedom."

Life! Life! Life will live!

MINISTER: Never! Death is all!

JOAN: Colour is life! Colour is love!

MINISTER: Never! All is black!

JOAN's music overpowers the MINISTER. The MINISTER stumbles backward, weakening.

JOAN: I sign!
My heart beats hard!
Feel my heartbeat!
Free us all!
Death is gone!
My love! My love!
Love! Love! Love! Love!
Love is freedom!

JOAN signs with a desperate and beautiful fury—

The drumbeat builds to a frenzy until—

Scene Ten

Same place: the valley.

The sky explodes in a brilliant flash of white light.

As the light fades, the world fills with colour. The landscape is green and vibrant. The statues wave and walk away. Birds fly through the sky.

The MINISTER, *defeated, is forced away off stage, completely closed off from this world. He is no longer in power.*

The BUTTERFLY, *the* BULLDOG, AVA, *and* SQUIB *embrace each other, celebrating.*

KAREN *snaps out of her stupor. She sees* JOAN.

JOAN *and* KAREN *approach each other.* JOAN *takes* KAREN*'s hands and caresses* KAREN*'s face.*

They kiss. A long, beautiful kiss of relief, of comfort, of the enduring strength of love.

JOAN: We're together again.

KAREN: You can't stay here.

JOAN: Why not? What's life if I can't be with the one I love?

KAREN: I'll still be here when the time comes. You need to take your music to the world.

JOAN: I need you.

KAREN: The world needs your voice. Your music. You need to let me go.

JOAN: After all this . . .

KAREN: I know.

JOAN: I love you.

KAREN: I love you.

JOAN kisses KAREN's hands. They part ways.

AVA, BUTTERFLY, BULLDOG, SQUIB: Music?

JOAN: Music?

The rest of the cast (chorus) signs along with JOAN.

What Is Music (Reprise)

JOAN & CHORUS:
Signed music
Throw away the old ways, the old sign . . .
There's a new sign! Signed Music!

Production's new sign for "Signed Music."

Earthquake!
Music!

BUTTERFLY: *(solo)* Butterflies grow
They always fly
They're always free
My friend, I'll always support you
Always cherish you
I love you all

BULLDOG: *(runs up the lineup, solo)*
These are my friends!
I'm loyal, I cherish them all
Though I may look like a bad dog,
I'm a big good bulldog!

AVA: *(solo)* We love, we inspire, we wave
We laugh
We come together
We change the world
We dance
Show the world who we are!

SQUIB: *(solo)* No more oppression, I'm free!
No longer alone
We're all together
We're free
The black heart is gone

CHORUS: All together
The world changes
And makes an earthquake!

JOAN dances with each character in turn:

BUTTERFLY: *(dance solo)* Love you all!

CHORUS: All!

SQUIIB: *(dance solo)* The black heart is gone!

CHORUS: Gone!

AVA: *(dance solo)* We change the world!

CHORUS: The world!

BULLDOG: *(dance solo)* Loyal to the end!

CHORUS: Loyal!

JOAN: Into the new world we jump
We dive, headfirst
We swim through the world
Leaving the music of ripples
We swim through the sky
Touching the stars
Our hearts bloom
Our beauty grows
In Signed Music
In music
Music
Music!

Everyone except JOAN *begin to slowly back off stage.* JOAN *exits last.*

Scene Eleven

The In-Between Land fades away.

A white tunnel like the black tunnel in Scene Three develops around JOAN, *enveloping her, taking her back to the cemetery.*

Green grass. Bright sun. Headstones.

JOAN *stands before* KAREN*'s grave.* KAREN *floats across the stage, smiling softly. She exudes peace, harmony, love. She passes* JOAN, *then floats away.*

A tree—perhaps the same tree that spoke to JOAN *earlier—watches* JOAN. *It smiles a little, offering a little comfort. It is relaxed, at peace; its limbs are no longer tight and on edge.*

JOAN *performs the last piece of Signed Music—*

JOAN: Love is too big . . .
The light is too bright . . .

Fade to black.

Scene Twelve

A rumble of drums.

A streak of black lightning—

The MINISTER *appears on stage. He addresses the audience—*

MINISTER: I'll find other people to break. There are always others. Not everybody's as strong as you. I'll always be here. I'll always be a part of life.

The MINISTER *vanishes.*

Curtain.

Acknowledgements

First, to Annie, Blake, and the Playwrights Canada Press staff for shepherding my script onto bookshelves.
To the Canada Council for funding the initial production in 2019.
To Soulpepper Theatre for staging the play's initial run.
To Clin d'Oeil for including the play in its summer festival.
To Joanne Cripps for making the initial overture back in 2016.
To Ann, Shay, and Jack for coming to see the play on opening night.
To Brad Fraser, theatre mentor and friend.
To Bob, Dawn, Daniel, Corinna, Yan, Courage, Agata, Abbey, Sita, and Jaelyn, who gave the characters heartbeats.
To Sølvi and Mira, who introduced me to the beautiful city of Oslo.
To Maryam, whose friendship has buoyed me on multiple occasions.
Most of all, to Deb. For everything.

Born Deaf and raised in a hearing family, Adam Pottle is the award-winning author of works in multiple genres, including the acclaimed writing memoir *Voice* and the horror novel *Apparitions*. His plays include the groundbreaking works *Ultrasound* and *The Black Drum*; he was the 2021–22 writer-in-residence at Sheridan College and a 2022 Warner Bros. Discovery Access screenwriting fellow. When not writing, he can be found at the boxing gym, the library, or the park with his wife Deborah and their goldendoodle Valkyrie. He lives in Saskatoon.